# The Startup Risk Management Handbook

A Practical Guide for Building a Resilient Business

# MALIYE NKHOMA

SUCCESS HIVE PRINT

# Contents

Foreword:

- Why You Shouldn't Fear the Unknown in Your Startup Journey

Introduction:

- The Startup Roll-coaster and Why You Need a Seatbelt

Part 1: The Risk Landscape for Startups

- 1: Identifying Your Startup's Kryptonite: Common Startup Risks.
- 2: From Minor Hiccup to Major Disaster: Assessing Risk Severity

Part 2: Building Your Startup's Defenses: Strategies for Risk Management

- 3: Dodge, Dip, Duck, Dive, Dodge! Strategies to Avoid Risks Entirely

- 4: When Avoidance Isn't an Option: Strategies to Mitigate Risks

- 5: When Disaster Strikes: Preparing for Recovery

Part 3: Risk Management Made Easy: Tools and Resources for Startups

- 6: Simple Tools for Big Results: Risk Management Templates and Checklists

- 7: Staying Ahead of the Curve: Keeping Your Risk Management Up-to-Date.

Conclusion

Bonus Chapter

# Forehead

### Why You Shouldn't Fear the Unknown in Your Startup Journey

Imagine this: you've poured your heart and soul into your startup idea. You've got a brilliant product, a passionate team, and a burning desire to make it big. But then, out of nowhere, WHAM! A global pandemic disrupts your supply chain. Or maybe a competitor launches a near-identical product, stealing your market share. Suddenly, your dream feels more like a nightmare.

This, my friend, is the land of unexpected challenges – the territory of risks. And let's be honest, risks can be unpredictable. They wrinkle your forehead (figuratively, of course) and make you sweat. But what if I told you that facing these risks head-on is the key to building a thriving, sustainable startup? That's where risk management comes in.

Think of risk management as a superhero cape for your startup. It equips you with the tools and knowledge to anticipate potential problems, so you're not left scrambling when they inevitably arise. This book is your guide to becoming a risk management superhero, ready to conquer the unknown and build a business that lasts.

So, take a deep breath, smooth out that furrowed brow, and dive into the world of startup survival! We're about to embark on a journey that will turn fear of the unknown into the fuel that propels your startup to success.

# Introduction

**The Startup Rollercoaster and Why You Need a Seatbelt**

Have you ever dreamt of launching your own business? Of being your own boss and turning your innovative idea into a reality? If so, then welcome to the exciting, exhilarating, and sometimes downright terrifying world of startups!

It's a rollercoaster ride, for sure. One minute you're celebrating a major milestone, the next you're facing a seemingly insurmountable challenge; A key employee quits unexpectedly. A competitor launches a product eerily similar to yours. Suddenly, your carefully crafted business plan feels like a crumpled piece of paper in a windstorm.

These unexpected bumps and turns are what we call risks. They're the hidden corners of the startup journey that can throw you off balance if you're not prepared. The good news? You can be.

This book is your guide to understanding and managing risks in your startup. We won't drown you in complicated jargon or financial mumbo jumbo. Instead, we'll break down the essentials in plain English, so even the most risk-averse entrepreneur can feel empowered to take control.

**Here's what you'll discover:**

- The different types of risks that can lurk around every corner for your startup.
- How to identify and assess these risks before they become major headaches.
- Practical strategies to avoid some risks altogether and mitigate the impact of others.
- Essential tools and resources to keep your risk management plan up-to-date.
-

By the end of this book, you'll be a risk management pro, ready to navigate the twists and turns of the startup journey with confidence. So, buckle up, grab your metaphorical seatbelt, and let's build a startup that thrives, not just survives!

# Part 1
# The Risk Landscape for Startups

# 1

## Identifying Your Startup's Kryptonite: Common Startup Risks

Congratulations! You've taken the plunge and embarked on your exciting startup journey. You've got a brilliant idea, a passionate team, and the drive to make a real difference. But the road to success is rarely smooth. Just like Superman has his kryptonite, every startup faces its own unique set of challenges – the unexpected obstacles that can derail your progress. These challenges, my friend, are what we call risks.

### What are Startup Risks?

In the world of business, a risk is anything that could potentially threaten your startup's success. It can be a financial setback, a legal hurdle, a sudden shift in the market, or even an internal operational issue. The key thing to remember is that risks are inevitable. They're like unexpected bumps on the road – you can't avoid them entirely, but you can certainly prepare for them.

### Why Should You Care About Startup Risks?

Let's face it, ignoring risks is a recipe for disaster. Many startups fail because they simply weren't prepared for the curveballs life threw their way. Maybe they underestimated the competition, or perhaps they ran out of cash before their product gained traction.

Whatever the case, a lack of risk management can turn a promising idea into a cautionary tale.

## The Benefits of Risk Management

The good news is that you don't have to be a superhero to conquer risk. By taking a proactive approach to risk management, you can significantly improve your startup's chances of success. Here are just a few benefits:

- **Increased Resilience:** A strong risk management plan equips you to face challenges with confidence. You'll be able to anticipate potential problems and develop contingency plans to minimize their impact.
- **Improved Decision-Making:** Risk management forces you to think critically about your business and its vulnerabilities. This leads to more informed decisions that can safeguard your startup's future.
- **Enhanced Investor Confidence:** Businesses that demonstrate a proactive approach to risk management are more attractive to investors. They see it as a sign of maturity and responsibility, making your startup a more compelling investment proposition.

## A Landscape of Risks: Common Threats Faced by Startups

Now that you understand why risk management is crucial, let's delve into the specific challenges that startups commonly face. Here are some of the most frequent risk categories:

- **Financial Risks:** This category encompasses everything related to the financial health of your startup. It includes running out of cash, failing to secure funding, unexpected expenses, and poor budgeting.

- **Market Risks:** These risks stem from external market forces that can impact your business. Examples include changes in customer preferences, new regulations, economic downturns, and intense competition.
- **Operational Risks:** These are internal issues that can disrupt your day-to-day operations. This could be anything from inefficient processes to employee turnover, technological breakdowns, or inadequate quality control.
- **Legal Risks:** Startups often face legal challenges, such as intellectual property infringement lawsuits, contractual disputes, or non-compliance with regulations.
- **Strategic Risks:** These risks relate to the overall direction and vision of your startup. It could include making the wrong decisions about product development, entering the wrong market at the wrong time, or failing to adapt to changing industry trends.

**Identifying Your Startup's Specific Risks**

While these categories provide a good starting point, it's important to identify the specific risks that are most relevant to your unique venture. Here are some questions to get you started:

- What type of product or service are you offering?
- Who is your target market?
- What is your competitive landscape?
- What stage of development are you in (e.g., idea stage, prototype stage, launch stage)?
- What are your funding sources?

By answering these questions, you can start to paint a clearer picture of the potential threats your startup faces.

## Real-World Examples: Bringing Risks to Life

Let's see how these risks can manifest in real-life startup scenarios:

- **Financial Risk:** A food delivery startup experiences a cash flow crunch due to a sudden increase in delivery driver fees.
- **Market Risk:** A social media app faces a major setback after a new privacy regulation restricts its ability to collect user data.
- **Operational Risk:** A clothing e-commerce store suffers a website outage during peak holiday shopping season due to a technical glitch.
- **Legal Risk:** A fitness tracker startup gets sued by a competitor for alleged patent infringement.
- **Strategic Risk:** A ride-sharing company focuses on expanding into a new city too quickly, neglecting to adapt its marketing strategy to the local audience.

**Remember:** Identifying your startup's specific risks is the first step towards effective risk management. By understanding your vulnerabilities, you can develop a plan to mitigate them and leaving you vulnerable to a world where even the most seemingly harmless banana peel can bring your entrepreneurial dreams crashing down. But fear not! This book is your guide to navigating the often-treacherous terrain of startup risks, equipping you with the knowledge and tools to dodge the proverbial banana peels and emerge victorious.

# 2

## From Minor Hiccup to Major Disaster: Assessing Risk Severity

In Chapter 1, we explored the various risks that lurk around every corner for your startup. Now, it's time to move from awareness to assessment. Just like a doctor wouldn't prescribe medication without a diagnosis, we can't develop a risk management plan without understanding the severity of each risk.

**Why Assess Risk Severity?**

Not all risks are created equal. Some pose a minor nuisance, while others hold the potential to derail your entire business. Imagine a leaky faucet versus a burst pipe. Both are issues, but clearly, the burst pipe requires a much more urgent and strategic response. By assessing risk severity, you can:

- **Prioritize effectively:** Focus your resources and attention on the risks that have the greatest potential impact on your startup.
- **Allocate resources wisely:** Invest in mitigation strategies for high-severity risks, while potentially accepting or monitoring lower-severity ones.

- **Develop contingency plans:** Create clear action plans to deal with the most critical risks, ensuring a swift and effective response when they materialize.

**The Art of Risk Assessment: A Two-Factor Approach**

The severity of a risk is determined by two key factors:

- **Likelihood:** How probable is it that the risk will actually occur?
- **Impact:** If the risk does occur, how badly will it affect your startup?

Let's break down each factor and explore how to assess them for your startup's specific risks.

**Factor 1: Likelihood - How Likely is the Risk to Occur?**

When assessing the likelihood of a risk, you're essentially trying to predict the future (admittedly, not an exact science!). However, by taking a data-driven and informed approach, you can develop a realistic picture of the risk's probability. Here are some questions to guide your assessment:

- **Industry Trends:** Has this risk impacted similar startups in your industry? How frequently did it occur?
- **Historical Data:** Has your startup experienced similar issues in the past? If so, how often?
- **External Factors:** Are there any external trends or circumstances that could increase the likelihood of the risk? (e.g., upcoming legislative changes, economic forecasts)
- **Control Measures:** Have you implemented any controls that might mitigate the likelihood of the risk? (e.g., cybersecurity protocols, diversified funding sources)

**Likelihood Scoring:**

Once you've considered these factors, assign a score to the likelihood of the risk occurring. A common approach is to use a scale like this:

- **Low (1-3):** Unlikely to occur, may require minimal monitoring.
- **Medium (4-6):** Somewhat likely to occur, warrants closer attention and potential mitigation strategies.
- **High (7-10):** Highly likely to occur, requires a robust mitigation plan and contingency actions.

**Factor 2: Impact - How Badly Could This Risk Hurt Your Startup?**

Now, let's turn our attention to the potential impact of the risk. Here, you want to consider the consequences of the risk materializing. How could it damage your startup's financial health, reputation, operations, or future prospects? Here are some key areas to consider:

- **Financial Impact:** How much money could your startup lose if the risk occurs? Consider lost sales, increased expenses, or legal penalties.
- **Operational Impact:** Could the risk disrupt your day-to-day operations? This could include delays in production, employee turnover, or customer service issues.
- **Reputational Impact:** Would the risk damage your brand image? This could lead to lost customer trust, negative media coverage, or difficulty attracting partners.
- **Strategic Impact:** Could the risk derail your long-term goals? This could involve missing critical market opportunities or having to pivot your entire business model.

**Impact Scoring:**

Similar to likelihood, assign a score to the potential impact of the risk using a scale like this:

- **Low (1-3):** Minor consequences, unlikely to significantly impact your startup.
- **Medium (4-6):** Moderate consequences, could cause some disruption or financial loss.
- **High (7-10):** Severe consequences, could threaten the survival or viability of your startup.

**The Risk Matrix: Putting It All Together**

Now that you've assessed both likelihood and impact, it's time to combine them to determine the overall risk severity. A common tool used for this purpose is the risk matrix. It's a simple grid where the likelihood scores are plotted on the horizontal axis and the impact scores on the vertical axis. Each intersection on the grid represents a specific risk with its corresponding severity level (usually categorized as Low, Medium, or High).

# Part 2

# Building Your Startup's Defenses: Strategies for Risk Management

# 3

**Dodge, Dip, Duck, Dive, Dodge! Strategies to Avoid Risks Entirely**

Imagine this: you're walking down a busy street, minding your own business, when you see a giant banana peel right in front of you. What do you do? Well, ideally, you'd avoid stepping on it altogether, right?

The same principle applies to risk management for startups. In a perfect world, we'd eliminate all potential threats before they can cause any damage. While that's not always possible, there are certainly strategies you can employ to avoid certain risks entirely. This chapter explores these proactive techniques, empowering you to dodge the proverbial banana peels on your startup journey.

**The Art of Risk Avoidance: Taking Control of Your Destiny**

Risk avoidance is all about proactive strategies that prevent the risk from occurring in the first place. This approach is often the most cost-effective and time-efficient way to manage risk. Here are some key strategies you can use:

### 1. Choosing the Right Path: Selecting a Low-Risk Business Model

Sometimes, the best way to avoid a risk is to simply not engage in activities that carry that risk. This might involve:

- **Choosing a stable industry:** Consider industries with a history of steady growth and low volatility.
- **Focusing on a niche market:** Catering to a specific audience can reduce competition and market uncertainty.
- **Adopting a bootstrapping approach:** Self-funding your startup minimizes dependence on external funding sources, reducing financial risks.

### 2. Partnering for Success: Leveraging Expertise to Mitigate Risks

Teaming up with experienced partners can help you avoid risks you might not even be aware of. Consider:

- **Outsourcing specialized tasks:** Hiring experts for legal, financial, or technological tasks can minimize risks associated with these areas.
- **Building strategic partnerships:** Collaborating with established companies can provide access to resources and expertise, reducing market risks.

**3. Planning for the Unforeseen: Building Flexibility into Your Operations**

Even the most meticulously planned startup can encounter unexpected situations. Here's how to be prepared:

- **Developing a diversified supplier network:** Relying on a single supplier can expose you to disruption if they experience issues.
- **Maintaining a cash flow buffer:** Having a financial cushion allows you to weather unexpected expenses or temporary setbacks.
- **Creating a remote work policy:** Offering remote work options can minimize operational risks associated with office closures or natural disasters.

**4. Prioritizing Quality: Building a Solid Foundation to Minimize Risks**

Cutting corners might seem like a way to save money in the short term, but it can lead to bigger problems down the road. Here's how to prioritize quality:

- **Investing in rigorous testing:** Thoroughly test your product or service before launch to minimize the risk of bugs or functionality issues.
- **Hiring qualified employees:** Invest in hiring and training the right talent to ensure a competent and reliable workforce.
- **Implementing strong security protocols:** Robust cybersecurity measures can prevent costly data breaches or cyberattacks.

## A Visual Representation: The Risk Matrix

Remember the risk matrix introduced in Chapter 2? This tool plays a crucial role in risk avoidance strategies. Here's a visual representation of a typical risk matrix:

## Risk Matrix Graph

| Likelihood      | Low (1-3)              | Medium (4-6)           | High (7-10)         |
| --------------- | ---------------------- | ---------------------- | ------------------- |
| Impact (1-3)    | Low Severity           | Low-Medium Severity    | Medium Severity     |
| Impact (4-6)    | Low-Medium Severity    | Medium Severity        | High Severity       |
| Impact (7-10)   | Medium Severity        | High Severity          | Very High Severity  |

**Utilizing the Risk Matrix for Avoidance:**

When assessing a risk, plot it on the risk matrix based on its likelihood and impact scores. Focus your avoidance efforts on risks that fall into the high likelihood/high impact quadrant.

For example, imagine a risk like "data breach" has a high likelihood score (it's fairly common for startups) and a high impact score (could result in financial losses and reputational damage). This risk would be a prime candidate for risk avoidance strategies like implementing strong cybersecurity protocols.

**The Benefits of Risk Avoidance**

By actively avoiding risks, you can reap several benefits:

- **Reduced Costs:** Prevention is always cheaper than cure. Avoiding risks can save you money down the line by preventing costly disruptions or legal issues.
- **Enhanced Efficiency:** By eliminating potential roadblocks, you can streamline your operations and focus on growing your business.
- **Improved Morale:** A proactive approach to risk management fosters a sense of security and stability within your team, leading to higher morale and productivity.

# 4

**When Avoidance Isn't an Option: Strategies to Mitigate Risks**

In the previous chapter, we explored the art of risk avoidance – the ultimate goal of any risk management strategy. But let's face it, not every risk can be completely eliminated. Sometimes, the banana peel is just too darn big to dodge entirely! This chapter dives into risk mitigation strategies – techniques to lessen the impact of a risk even if it does occur.

**The Reality of Risk: When Avoidance Falls Short**

While avoidance is ideal, some risks are simply unavoidable. For example, economic downturns happen, competitors emerge, and technology evolves – these are realities of the business world. The key here is to mitigate these risks, meaning you take steps to reduce their severity should they materialize.

**A Menu of Mitigation Strategies: Tailored Solutions for Different Risks**

There's no one-size-fits-all approach to risk mitigation. The most effective strategy depends on the specific risk you're facing. Here's a look at some common mitigation techniques:

## 1. Risk Transfer: Sharing the Burden

Sometimes, the best way to manage a risk is to transfer the responsibility to someone else. Here are some ways to achieve this:

- **Insurance:** Purchase insurance policies to protect your startup from financial losses due to events like property damage, liability lawsuits, or employee injuries.
- **Outsourcing:** Outsource high-risk activities to companies specializing in those areas, like data security or legal compliance.
- **Warranties:** Offer warranties or guarantees on your products or services to mitigate customer dissatisfaction and potential returns.

## 2. Risk Reduction: Minimizing the Potential Damage

Even if you can't completely avoid a risk, you can often take steps to reduce its potential impact. Here are some ways to achieve this:

- **Contingency Planning:** Develop a clear plan outlining how you'll respond to specific risks. This could include backup plans for supply chain disruptions, communication strategies for PR crises, or disaster recovery protocols.
- **Diversification:** Don't put all your eggs in one basket. Diversify your product offerings, funding sources, and customer base to minimize the impact of any single risk.
- **Invest in Security:** Implement strong security measures to protect your data, intellectual property, and infrastructure from cyberattacks.

## 3. Risk Retention: Accepting and Managing the Risk

For certain low-impact risks, the most cost-effective approach might be to simply accept them and manage the consequences as they arise. Here are some considerations:

- **Cost-Benefit Analysis:** Weigh the potential cost of the risk against the resources required to mitigate it. Sometimes, the cost of mitigation outweighs the potential impact of the risk itself.
- **Self-Insurance:** If you have a strong cash flow buffer, you might choose to self-insure against certain low-probability risks.
- **Monitoring and Adapting:** Continuously monitor accepted risks and be prepared to adjust your approach if the impact becomes more severe than anticipated.

**A Visual Representation: The Risk Treatment Matrix**

Now that we've explored various mitigation strategies, let's introduce the risk treatment matrix. This tool helps you select the most appropriate mitigation strategy for a particular risk.

Risk Treatment Matrix Graph

| Likelihood | Avoid | Transfer | Reduce | Accept |
|---|---|---|---|---|
| High Impact | Focus | Consider | Consider | Only as last resort |
| Medium Impact | Consider | Consider | Focus | Consider |
| Low Impact | May be possible | Consider | May be possible | Focus |

## Utilizing the Risk Treatment Matrix for Mitigation

Plot your risk on the risk matrix based on its likelihood and impact scores. The matrix highlights the most appropriate mitigation strategy based on the risk's severity.

For example, a risk like "key employee leaving" might have a medium likelihood (it happens, but not all the time) and a high impact (could disrupt operations significantly). According to the matrix, the focus should be on reduction strategies like cross-training employees or establishing strong retention programs.

## Additional Considerations for Effective Mitigation

Here are some additional tips for effective risk mitigation:

- **Develop a Risk Management Culture:** Foster a company culture where everyone is aware of potential risks and actively participates in mitigation efforts.
- **Regularly Review and Update:** The business landscape is constantly changing, so revisit your risk assessments and mitigation plans regularly.
- **Communication is Key:** Ensure clear communication with all stakeholders regarding potential risks and mitigation plans.

## Mitigating Risks: Building Resilience for Your Startup

By implementing a robust risk mitigation strategy, you equip your startup with the tools and mindset to navigate the unexpected twists and turns of the entrepreneurial journey. Here's how a well-defined mitigation plan fosters resilience within your company:

**Increased Preparedness:** Having a plan in place means you're not scrambling to react when a risk materializes. A clear mitigation strategy allows for a swift and effective response, minimizing disruption and potential damage.

**Enhanced Confidence:** Knowing you have a plan in place to address potential challenges builds confidence within your team. Employees feel empowered to tackle obstacles and overcome setbacks, fostering a more proactive and solution-oriented environment.

**Improved Adaptability:** Risk mitigation strategies often involve building redundancies and flexibility into your operations. This allows your startup to adapt to changing circumstances and unforeseen events, ensuring business continuity even in the face of disruption.

**Stronger Decision Making:** The process of identifying, assessing, and mitigating risks encourages a thoughtful approach to decision-making. You consider potential consequences alongside potential rewards, leading to more informed and strategic choices.

### The Ripple Effect of Risk Mitigation:

The benefits of a robust risk mitigation strategy extend beyond your startup. By proactively managing risks, you contribute to a healthier entrepreneurial ecosystem:

**Investor Confidence:** Investors are more likely to back startups that demonstrate a proactive approach to risk management. A well-defined mitigation plan showcases your commitment to long-term sustainability and reduces the perceived risk of their investment.

**Industry Collaboration:** As more startups prioritize risk management, opportunities for collaboration and knowledge sharing increase. Learning from each other's experiences strengthens the entire entrepreneurial community.

**Overall Market Stability:** By mitigating risks and ensuring the success of startups, you contribute to a more stable and predictable business environment, fostering long-term economic growth.

# 5

**When Disaster Strikes: Preparing for Recovery**

Even with the best risk management strategies in place, unexpected events can still occur. Imagine this: a critical supplier goes bankrupt, a competitor launches a near-identical product, or a global pandemic disrupts your entire industry. These are the moments where your startup's true resilience is tested.

This chapter focuses on recovery planning – the essential steps you can take to bounce back from unforeseen challenges and ensure your startup's survival.

**The Aftermath of a Crisis: Picking Up the Pieces**

Let's face it, crises happen. The key is to be prepared to respond effectively and minimize the long-term damage. Here's what to expect when a risk materializes:

- **Initial Disruption:** The immediate impact of the risk will likely cause some level of disruption to your business operations. This could involve lost revenue, production delays, or reputational damage.

- **Decision Making Under Pressure:** You and your team will need to make critical decisions quickly and efficiently to contain the damage and chart a course for recovery.
- **Uncertainty and Anxiety:** Crises can create a sense of uncertainty and anxiety within your team. Effective communication and leadership are crucial to maintain morale and focus.

## The Power of Preparation: Building a Recovery Plan

While you can't predict every unforeseen event, you can certainly prepare for the unknown unknowns. Developing a comprehensive recovery plan is your secret weapon for navigating crisis situations.

**Here's a step-by-step guide to building a robust recovery plan:**

1. **Identify Potential Crises:** Brainstorm and list down the most critical risks your startup faces. Think beyond financial risks and consider operational disruptions, PR crises, or legal issues.

2. **Define Response Teams:** Assign specific roles and responsibilities for each potential crisis. Form dedicated teams with clear decision-making authority to handle different scenarios.

3. **Develop Communication Strategies:** Outline a communication plan for different stakeholders – employees, customers, investors, and the media. Define who will communicate what, when, and how.

4. **Establish Backup Systems:** Create contingency plans for essential business functions. This could involve having a backup supplier network, a disaster recovery plan for your IT infrastructure, or alternative customer service channels.

5. **Conduct Regular Reviews and Drills:** Don't let your recovery plan gather dust on a shelf! Schedule regular reviews to update it as your business evolves. Conduct crisis simulation exercises to test your team's response and identify areas for improvement.

## A Case Study: How a Startup Bounced Back from Disaster

Let's see how a well-defined recovery plan can make a difference in real life. Imagine a food delivery startup called "Fresh Bites." Their business relies heavily on a network of independent delivery drivers. One day, a new law is passed that reclassifies these drivers as employees, significantly increasing Fresh Bites' labor costs.

Without a recovery plan, this could have been a crippling blow. However, Fresh Bites had anticipated this risk and developed a mitigation strategy. Here's how their recovery plan helped them navigate the crisis:

- **Activation of Response Team:** The designated crisis team, led by the COO, immediately convened to assess the situation and develop a response.
- **Communication with Drivers:** Fresh Bites proactively communicated the new regulations to their driver network, explaining the impact and exploring potential solutions.
- **Negotiating with Platforms:** The company negotiated with food delivery platforms they partnered with to share the increased costs associated with the new regulations.
- **Optimizing Operations:** Fresh Bites reviewed their delivery routes and implemented route optimization software to improve efficiency and reduce overall delivery costs.

By implementing their pre-defined recovery plan, Fresh Bites not only mitigated the impact of the new regulations but also emerged from the crisis stronger and more efficient.

**Beyond Recovery: Building a Culture of Resilience**

Recovery planning goes beyond just having a document. It's about fostering a culture of resilience within your startup. Here are some tips to achieve this:

- **Embrace a "Learn from Failure" Mentality:** View setbacks as learning opportunities and use them to improve your risk management strategies for the future.
- **Empower Your Team:** Build a team that's comfortable making decisions and taking initiative, especially during critical situations.
- **Invest in Crisis Leadership Training:** Equip your leadership team with the skills and knowledge to navigate crisis situations effectively.

# Part 3

# Risk Management Made Easy: Tools and Resources for Startups

# 6

## Simple Tools for Big Results: Risk Management Templates and Checklists

Congratulations! You've journeyed through the world of startup risk management, learning the essential strategies to navigate the unexpected. Now it's time to put theory into practice. This chapter equips you with the practical tools you need to implement a robust risk management plan for your startup.

## From Knowledge to Action: Making Risk Management a Reality

While understanding risk management principles is crucial, the real power lies in applying them to your specific startup. This chapter provides you with a collection of downloadable templates and checklists designed to simplify the risk management process.

**These tools will help you:**

- Identify and assess potential risks specific to your startup.

- Develop clear and actionable mitigation strategies.
- Monitor and update your risk management plan as your business evolves.

**Template 1: Risk Identification Brainstorming Sheet**

Download Link: Risk Identification Brainstorming Sheet: link to downloadable template

This template helps you brainstorm and identify potential risks your startup might face. It's a collaborative exercise, best done with your team.

Instructions:

1. **List Your Business Activities:** Start by listing down all the key activities involved in your business operations. This could include product development, marketing, sales, customer service, etc.
2. **Identify Potential Issues:** For each activity, brainstorm and list down any potential challenges or issues that could arise. Think broadly, considering financial, operational, legal, market-related, and strategic risks.
3. **Rate the Impact and Likelihood:** For each potential risk, assign a score (low, medium, high) based on its likelihood of occurring and its potential impact on your business.

Example:

| Business Activity | Potential Risk | Likelihood (1-10) | Impact (1-10) |
|---|---|---|---|
| Product Development | Delay in product launch due to technical issues | Medium (5) | High (8) |
| Marketing | Negative social media campaign affecting brand reputation | Low (3) | Medium (6) |
| Sales | Difficulty securing funding from investors | High (7) | Very High (9) |

**Template 2: Risk Assessment Matrix**

Download Link: Risk Assessment Matrix: link to downloadable template

This template builds upon the information gathered in the Risk Identification Brainstorming Sheet. It helps you visualize the overall severity of each risk based on its likelihood and impact scores.

## Instructions:

1. **Transfer Information**: Transfer the identified risks, likelihood scores, and impact scores from the Brainstorming Sheet to the Risk Assessment Matrix.
2. **Plot the Risks**: Plot each risk on the matrix according to its likelihood and impact scores. This will position each risk in a specific quadrant representing its overall severity (low, medium, high).
3. **Prioritize Actions:** Focus your risk management efforts on the high-severity risks located in the top right quadrant of the matrix. These require immediate mitigation strategies.

### Risk Assessment Matrix:

| Likelihood | Low (1-3) | Medium (4-6) | High (7-10) |
|---|---|---|---|
| Impact (1-3) | Low Severity | Low-Medium Severity | Medium Severity |
| Impact (4-6) | Low-Medium Severity | Medium Severity | High Severity |
| Impact (7-10) | Medium Severity | High Severity | Very High Severity |

## Template 3: Risk Mitigation Action Plan

Download Link: Risk Mitigation Action Plan: link to downloadable template

This template helps you develop specific and actionable mitigation strategies for your identified risks.

**Instructions:**

1. **List High-Severity Risks**: Start by listing down the high-severity risks identified in the Risk Assessment Matrix. These are the priorities.
2. **Define Mitigation Strategies:** For each high-severity risk, brainstorm and list down potential mitigation strategies. Consider the options discussed in Chapter 4 (avoidance, transfer, reduction, acceptance).
3. **Assign Responsibilities:** Assign ownership for each mitigation strategy. Who will be responsible for implementing and monitoring the strategy?
4. **Set Timelines:** Establish a timeline for implementing each mitigation strategy.
5. **Track Progress:** Create a system for tracking the progress of your mitigation strategies. Are they effective in reducing the risk?

Example:

| Risk | Mitigation Strategy | Owner | Timeline |
|---|---|---|---|
| Delay in product launch | Implement rigorous testing procedures | Product Development Lead | Ongoing |
| Difficulty securing funding | Diversify funding sources (e.g., crowdfunding, angel investors) | CEO | Next Quarter |
| Data breach | Implement robust cybersecurity protocols (firewalls, data encryption) | IT Manager | Within |

# 7

**The Final Frontier: Integrating Risk Management into Your Startup Culture**

We've reached the final chapter of our exploration into the world of startup risk management. Throughout this journey, you've learned how to identify risks, assess their severity, and develop strategies to mitigate them. However, risk management isn't a one-time event; it's an ongoing process that needs to be deeply ingrained in your startup's culture.

**Why Integrate Risk Management into Your Culture?**

Think of your startup culture as the foundation of your business. A strong foundation built on risk awareness and preparedness allows you to weather any storm. Here are some key benefits of integrating risk management into your company's DNA:

- **Proactive Problem Solving:** When risk management becomes a cultural norm, your team becomes adept at identifying and addressing potential issues before they escalate.
- **Enhanced Decision Making:** A risk-aware culture encourages a thoughtful approach to decision-making, considering potential consequences alongside potential rewards.
- **Increased Transparency and Communication:** Open communication about risks fosters trust and collaboration within your team, leading to more effective mitigation strategies.
- **Improved Adaptability:** By anticipating challenges, your startup becomes more adaptable and resilient in the face of unexpected disruptions.

**Building a Risk-Aware Culture: Strategies for Long-Term Success**

So, how do you transform risk management from a checklist to a core value within your startup? Here are some practical steps:

**1. Lead by Example:**

As a leader, your commitment to risk management sets the tone for the entire company. Here's how to show your dedication:

- Actively participate in risk identification and assessment exercises.
- Allocate resources for implementing risk mitigation strategies.
- Communicate openly about risks and challenges with your team.

## 2. Foster a Culture of Learning:

Encourage your team to continuously learn and improve their risk management skills. Here's how to achieve this:

- Provide training workshops on risk identification and mitigation strategies.
- Share success stories of how risk management has helped the company navigate challenges.
- Encourage open discussions about potential risks and near misses.

## 3. Integrate Risk Management into Existing Processes:

Don't treat risk management as a separate task. Weave it into the fabric of your everyday operations:

- Incorporate risk assessments into project planning and budgeting processes.
- Establish regular risk review meetings to monitor and update your risk management plan.
- Empower employees to report potential risks without fear of repercussions.

## 4. Celebrate Risk Management Champions:

Recognize and reward employees who actively participate in risk identification and mitigation efforts. This motivates others to follow suit and reinforces the value of risk awareness.

## 5. Leverage Technology:

Several online tools and software applications can streamline your risk management process. Consider exploring these options to enhance efficiency and data-driven decision making.

**The Evolving Landscape of Risk:**

The business world is constantly evolving, and so are the risks your startup faces. Here are some additional considerations to keep in mind:

- **Emerging Technologies:** As technology advances, new risks and opportunities will arise. Stay informed about tech trends and their potential impact on your business.
- **The Changing Regulatory Environment:** Governments frequently enact new regulations that can impact various aspects of your business. Stay abreast of regulatory changes and adjust your risk management strategy accordingly.
- **Global Interdependence:** In today's interconnected world, events happening across the globe can impact your startup. Consider potential global risks when assessing your vulnerabilities.

# Conclusion

**Stepping into the Future with Confidence**

Congratulations! You've reached the culmination of your exploration into the world of startup risk management. Throughout this journey, you've equipped yourself with the knowledge and tools to navigate the inevitable challenges that lie ahead on your entrepreneurial path. Remember, the road to success for your startup is rarely smooth, but by embracing a proactive approach to risk management, you significantly increase your chances of reaching your destination.

As you embark on your real-world startup adventure, consider these key takeaways:

- **Risk Management is a Continuous Journey:** Building a resilient startup isn't a one-time event; it's an ongoing process. Regularly revisit your risk assessments, update

your mitigation strategies, and adapt to the ever-evolving business landscape.
- **Embrace the Power of Communication:** Open and transparent communication about potential risks and mitigation plans is crucial. Foster an environment where employees feel comfortable raising concerns and suggesting solutions.
- **Learn from Others and Share Your Knowledge:** The startup community is a valuable resource. Learn from the experiences of others who have navigated risk, and share your own challenges and successes to inspire and support fellow entrepreneurs.

**The Risk Management Mindset: A Recipe for Success**

Beyond the practical tools and techniques, risk management cultivates a specific mindset within your startup culture. This mindset emphasizes the following:

- **Proactive Problem Solving:** Instead of waiting for problems to arise, you anticipate potential issues and develop strategies to address them before they escalate.
- **Data-Driven Decision Making:** Decisions are grounded in facts and analysis, considering the potential risks and rewards associated with each option.
- **Adaptability and Resilience:** Your startup is prepared to bounce back from setbacks, learning from challenges and emerging stronger than before.
- **Embrace of Change:** The business world is constantly evolving, and a risk-aware culture readily adapts to new realities and emerging challenges.

**The Ripple Effect: Building a Stronger Ecosystem**

By integrating risk management into your startup's DNA, you don't just benefit your own company. You contribute to a healthier overall entrepreneurial ecosystem. When startups prioritize risk management, the following positive effects can be observed:

- **Increased Investor Confidence:** Investors are more likely to back startups that demonstrate a proactive approach to managing risk.
- **Collaboration and Knowledge Sharing:** As risk management practices become more widespread, startups can learn from each other's experiences, fostering a collaborative and supportive environment.
- **Innovation and Long-Term Growth:** By mitigating risks and ensuring sustainability, startups can focus on innovation and long-term growth, ultimately contributing to a more vibrant and resilient business landscape.

**A Final Note: The Power is in Your Hands**

The future of your startup is bright, and the power to navigate the challenges and seize the opportunities lies within your grasp. By embracing risk management and cultivating a culture of resilience, you empower your company to not only survive but thrive in the face of uncertainty. Remember, the journey is just as important as the destination. Enjoy the ride, learn from your experiences, and most importantly, never stop exploring and innovating. As the great Wayne Gretzky once said, "You miss 100% of the shots you don't take." So, take aim at your entrepreneurial dreams, manage your risks effectively, and watch your startup soar to new heights.

# Bonus Chapter

### Risk Management for the Solopreneur

The world of startups isn't limited to venture-backed, high-growth companies. Solopreneurs – individuals who launch and run their own businesses – are a vital part of the entrepreneurial ecosystem. While the scale and complexity of risks might differ, effective risk management is equally important for solopreneurs to ensure their ventures flourish.

### Tailoring the Approach: Risk Management for One

The strategies outlined in this book might seem geared towards larger teams. However, the core principles of risk management translate perfectly to the solopreneur world. Here's how to adapt the approach for your solo journey:

- **Identify Your Strengths and Weaknesses:** As a solopreneur, you wear many hats. Identify areas where you excel and areas where you might be more vulnerable. This self-awareness helps you pinpoint potential risks associated with your skillset.
- **Embrace Automation:** Technology can be your greatest ally. Utilize project management tools, communication platforms, and customer relationship management (CRM) software to streamline operations and free up your time to focus on strategic risk management.
- **Build Your Support Network:** The lack of a formal team doesn't mean you have to go it alone. Connect with other solopreneurs, join online communities, and seek mentorship from experienced individuals. Share challenges, exchange ideas, and learn from each other's risk management experiences.

**Common Risks Faced by Solopreneurs:**

While the specific risks will vary depending on your business model, here are some common challenges solopreneurs face:

- **Client Dependence:** Relying on a single or few clients can be risky. Diversify your client base to mitigate the impact of losing a major source of income.
- **Limited Resources:** Solopreneurs often have limited financial and time resources. Focus on high-impact activities that generate the most value and outsource tasks when possible.
- **Work-Life Balance:** The lines between work and personal life can easily blur for solopreneurs. Establish clear boundaries, schedule time for self-care, and avoid burnout.

**Risk Management Strategies for Solopreneurs:**

Here are some practical strategies you can implement to manage these common risks:

- **Develop Ironclad Contracts:** Clearly define the scope of work, payment terms, and termination clauses in your client contracts to protect yourself from misunderstandings and disputes.
- **Set Realistic Goals and Timelines:** Don't overload yourself. Plan achievable projects with realistic deadlines to avoid stress and potential burnout.
- **Prioritize Self-Care:** Schedule time for exercise, healthy meals, and breaks throughout the day. A healthy and well-rested solopreneur is a productive solopreneur.

**The Future of Solopreneurship: A Risk-Aware Landscape**

The solopreneur landscape is constantly evolving. Here are some emerging trends to keep in mind:

- **The Rise of the Freelancer Economy:** More and more individuals are choosing the freelance path. This creates a wealth of opportunities for solopreneurs to offer specialized skills and services.
- **The Power of Online Platforms:** Online platforms connect solopreneurs with a global audience, making it easier to find clients and market your services.
- **The Importance of Continuous Learning:** The business world is in flux, and staying updated with industry trends and new technologies is crucial for solopreneurs to remain competitive.

**Conclusion: The Solopreneur's Risk Management Toolkit**

By embracing risk management, solopreneurs can navigate the exciting yet challenging world of running their own businesses. Remember, the key is to:

- Identify your unique risks and vulnerabilities.
- Develop a plan to mitigate those risks, leveraging technology and building a support network.
- Continuously assess, adapt, and learn from your experiences.

With a proactive approach to risk management, you can transform your solopreneurship journey from a white-knuckled ride into a fulfilling and successful adventure. So, step out there, embrace the challenges, and watch your solo business soar!

www.ingramcontent.com/pod-product-compliance
Lightning Source LLC
Chambersburg PA
CBHW070948220526
45471CB00007B/2934